little black book

for graduates

by blaine bartel

little black book

for graduates

by blaine bartel

Harrison House
Tulsa, Oklahoma

06 05 04 03   10 9 8 7 6 5 4 3 2 1

Little Black Book for Graduates
ISBN 1-57794-612-X
Copyright © by Blaine Bartel
P.O. Box 691923
Tulsa, Oklahoma 74179

Published by Harrison House, Inc.
P.O. Box 35035
Tulsa, Oklahoma 74153

contents

Education

- 5 Things to Remember When Considering Secondary Education
- 4 Ways to Pursue a Scholarship
- 3 Qualities of a Great Learner
- 6 Things School Will Never Teach You
- 5 Steps to Educating Yourself
- 7 Books That Can Change Your Life
- 4 Surefire Ways to Discover Your Talents
- 3 Keys to Effective Planning

Career

- 4 Ways to Discover Your Life's Calling
- 3 Secrets to Real Success
- 5 Ways to Get a Great Job
- 3 Keys to Sound Career Decisions
- 6 Steps to Finding Favor in the Workplace
- 6 Keys to Being Promoted by Your Boss
- 3 Reasons to Quit Your Job
- 4 Kinds of People Who Constantly Get Fired

contents (continued)

Cash

- 4 Keys to Effective Budgeting and Saving
- 10 Questions to Spending Wisely
- 3 Reasons You Should Tithe
- 4 Things You Should Know About Investing
- 3 Places for Successful Investing
- 4 Reasons You Should Buy a House
- 5 Ways Money Can Destroy People
- 7 Rewards of the Giver

God

- 4 Steps to Finding Favor With God
- 3 Daily Habits to Grow in Your Relationship With God
- 3 Mistakes Graduates Make in Their Walk With God
- 7 Scriptures That Prove God Is Confident in You
- 3 Secrets to Answered Prayer
- 4 Ways God Gives You Direction
- 4 Reasons You Need a Pastor
- 5 Things God Says About Work

contents (continued)

[EDUCATION]

5 THINGS TO REMEMBER WHEN CONSIDERING SECONDARY EDUCATION

Choosing what to do after high school can be a big decision. Should I go to college, start working, or stay home and live off mom and dad for the rest of my life? I suggest one of the first two options as a more fulfilling and financially profitable choice.

Here are 5 things that will help you when considering secondary education.

1. **A college education can open more doors of opportunity.** Today, more and more employers are looking for college education as a qualification for even many entry-level positions. Without a degree many opportunities in medicine, law, finance, computers, and other professional fields can be very difficult to break into. This isn't to say you can't succeed without a

degree, but it may be a much more difficult climb to the top.

2. **Can you afford it?** It can be very difficult to start life after college with a huge burden of school debt. Could you save money and still get the education you need by taking your first two years at a community college then transferring to an affordable university?

3. **How will the school influence your spiritual life?** Is this school known for its massive party atmosphere, or is it respected for its educational focus? Don't put yourself in a position to compromise by selecting the wrong school. Check your motives for wanting to attend a particular school.

4. **How do your parents feel about the school you are considering?** God will give your parents wisdom to help you make good

decisions. They have been around the block a
few times in life, so save yourself the heartache
and listen to your parents' advice.

5. **Is there a good church you can attend
   while going to college?** Without a good
   church your chances of a strong spiritual life are
   slim to none. If you put God first in choosing
   your school, He will take care of adding everything to you. (Matt. 6:33.)

4 WAYS TO PURSUE A SCHOLARSHIP

With the ever-increasing cost of a college education it is more important than ever to work hard and smart for scholarships. Few people have a bank account full of unlimited college funds, so here are a few tips to help you land the extra money you need for school.

1. **See your school guidance counselor to help you assess what kind of scholarships might be available to you.** The sooner you can do this in your high school years the more time you have to take those extra classes or join the extracurricular clubs that open more scholarship doors.

2. **Hit the books.** The better your grades, the more scholarship opportunities will become available to you. Pay the price now and you can have fun and play later, but if you choose to slack off and play now, it will cost you later.

3. **Join extra curricular activities.** Colleges are looking for students who take the initiative and show signs of leadership.

4. **Become an expert at something.** I've met many students who have been given full scholarships because of their highly developed athletic ability. This didn't come just because they were talented, but because they were faithful to develop their gift every day. If you are not athletic you may be good in music, drama, or science. Look for a way to distinguish yourself. If you do, you may have schools fighting for you rather than you fighting for them.

3 QUALITIES OF A GREAT LEARNER

Just because you have a brain doesn't mean you are using it beyond daily bodily functions. God has gifted you with a mind—learn to use and develop it. Albert Einstein was a life-long learner. If you learn to be a life-long learner you will go far in life. The moment you stop learning is the day you begin to die. Here are 3 qualities that will make you a great learner.

1. **Ask questions.** Science is simply the art of asking lots of questions and searching for the answer. What questions are you asking? When you are around people who know more than you, ask them lots of questions. Then, shut up and listen.

2. **Be teachable.** Someone once said, "It's what you learn after you know it all that counts." Some people limit their potential because they have an unteachable spirit. There isn't anyone that knows

everything—except God (and last time I checked, you weren't Him). That means there's more for you to learn.

3. **Have Passion.** Great learners are passionate to grow. One time a student of philosophy asked his teacher how he could become a man of great wisdom. The teacher said, "Follow me and I will show you." The teacher waded into the ocean and the student followed him. The wise teacher then held his young pupil under water until the student began to kick and fight his way to the surface. The student gasping for air asked, "What did you do that for?" The wise teacher replied, "When you want wisdom as much as you wanted air you will find it."

Make it a habit of never going to sleep without having learned something new that day.

6 THINGS SCHOOL WILL
NEVER TEACH YOU

Graduating from school isn't the end of learning—or at least it shouldn't be. School can teach you many things about your chosen profession, but there are some very important things school will mostly likely never teach you. These things you must pursue on your own.

1. **Common sense.** It is amazing how many well-educated people do incredibly stupid things. You can be book smart and brain dead when it comes to common sense. The book of Proverbs is a great place to grow your common sense. Make a habit of reading a chapter of Proverbs every day.

2. **Living within your means.** In today's society success doesn't have to be real as long as the clothes you wear, the house you live in, and the car you drive says you have reached

the top of the success ladder. Many people are mortgaging their future by accumulating debt when they should be accumulating wealth. Delay instant gratification for true, long-term financial success.

3. **How to be happy with yourself.** Today happiness is based on competition. Are you better looking than so and so, or are you better dressed, or is your car cooler? Don't fall into this empty and vain comparison trap. Let your happiness be based on who you are in Christ and what He has created you to be. Your life won't be an emotional roller coaster because God never changes.

4. **Building a successful marriage.** According to the National Center for Health Statistics, nearly half of all marriages end in divorce. People spend months planning a wedding that lasts a few hours but spend no time planning how to make their

marriage last a lifetime. Read books about building a marriage that will stand through the storms of life with your fiancé before you get married.

5. **How to be a good parent.** Most of us learn our parenting skills from how our parents raised us. This can be good if our parents did a good job. Even then there are most likely things you would do differently. Decide how you want to raise your children and start studying books that will help you train them up. (Prov. 22:6.)

6. **The meaning of life.** The meaning of life can't be found in a school textbook. It can only be found in a personal relationship with your Creator. The closer you are to Him, the closer you are to fulfilling your life's purpose.

5 STEPS TO EDUCATING YOURSELF

Many successful people in life are self-educated. Abraham Lincoln taught himself by reading books while growing up in a rugged log cabin. You may not have all the formal education you would like, but that doesn't have to be an excuse to remain ignorant. You can teach yourself if you apply these 5 principles.

1. **Read, read, read.** No one in America has an excuse to remain uneducated. We have public libraries, bookstores on every corner, and many public service self-help programs. Find books that will help you grow in your areas of interests and read, read, read.

2. **Listen to tapes.** If you're like me you might find it hard to read all the books you would like. Many of today's books are also available on audiotapes and CDs and can be found at your

local bookstore. I enjoy getting biographies on tape because they are often so big and take a while to read. Also, order good teaching and preaching tapes from your church and Christian bookstores. Just about everyone spends time in the car. Take your drive time and turn it into growth time by listening to tapes.

3. **Attend conferences and seminars.** Don't pass up the opportunity to attend motivational and teaching seminars. These can be a great source of motivation and instruction. Tapes are good, but there is nothing like hearing a great speaker live and in person.

4. **Surround yourself with experts.** I pick friends who know more than me about some-thing—like organization, or they may have more knowledge about a certain area of the Bible. By surrounding myself with experts I learn and grow

by being around them. Remember, you become like those you associate with. Who are you hanging around?

5. **Learn something from everyone you meet.** Everyone you meet knows something you don't—maybe they know more about cooking, investing, fixing cars, or sports. Even if they have failed miserably in an area of life, you can learn from their mistakes.

7 BOOKS THAT CAN CHANGE YOUR LIFE

Here are 7 books that contain powerful truths and ideas that, when applied, have the potential to change your future. Although most of these are not necessarily Christian books, each of them contains powerful biblical principles. Don't buy and read them all at once, but start checking them out one at a time.

1. *Sam Walton—Made in America* by Sam Walton: the inspiring story of a regular guy who built Wal-Mart.

2. *The 7 Habits of Highly Effective People* by Steven Covey: a bestseller for many years.

3. *Developing the Leader Within You* by John Maxwell: a guide to moving up the leadership ladder.

4. *The Millionaire Next Door* by Thomas J. Stanley and William D. Danko: the surprising secrets of America's wealthy.

5. *Rich Dad—Poor Dad* by Robert T. Kiyosaki: what the rich teach their kids about money that the poor and middle class do not.

6. *The Heart of a Leader* by Ken Blanchard: insights on the art of influence.

7. *How to Win Friends and Influence People* by Dale Carnegie: keys to winning in your relationships with people.

4 SUREFIRE WAYS TO
DISCOVER YOUR TALENTS

Proverbs 18:16 NKJV says, "A man's gift makes room for him, and brings him before great men." The discovery and implementation of your gifts and talents will bring you the success your heart desires.

Here are 4 ways to uncover your talents.

1. Ask those you know and trust what they see as your greatest talents.

2. Pray and ask God to reveal your gifts and talents to you. Jeremiah 33:3 promises that if we call on God, He'll show us hidden things which we don't know about.

3. Follow your heart's desires, and try new things. The results may surprise you.

4. Be faithful in little things you're asked to do, even if they aren't on your list of favorites. God tells us that if we're faithful in small things, we will be rulers over much. (Matt. 25:23.)

3 KEYS TO EFFECTIVE PLANNING

If you want success, you must plan for it. Someone
once asked Wayne Gretzky how he became the best goal
scorer in the history of hockey. He replied, "While
everyone else is chasing the puck, I go to where the
puck is going to be." He planned ahead. Let's take a
look at 3 keys to effective planning.

1. **Prayer.** You may not know what the future
   holds, but God does. God promises that if you
   will ask Him, He will show you things that you
   could never figure out on your own. (Jer. 33:3.)

2. **Goal setting.** Write out exactly what it is you
   are planning for. You will be amazed how this key
   will unlock your future.

3. **Prioritizing.** You can't keep your priorities if
   you don't have any. Putting things in order will

help you plan for and accomplish the most
important things first.

[CAREER]

4 WAYS TO DISCOVER YOUR
LIFE'S CALLING

Studies have proven again and again that people succeed most in doing what they love best. If you can accurately determine what you were created by God to do, you will truly find a life you will love living. Here are 4 ways to uncover the calling God has on your life.

1. **Delight yourself in the Lord. (Ps. 37:4.)** If you take joy in pursuing your personal relationship with Christ each day, the Bible promises that God will put His desires, drive, and passion in your life.

2. **Don't be afraid to try new things.** Take some risks. Try different kinds of activities, work, and projects. You may find something you're good at that no one knew about, including you.

3. **Ask for counsel from people you trust.**
   (Prov. 11:14.) The Bible says in a multitude of
   counsel there is safety. Ask those close to you
   with a track record of success what they see you
   being able to excel at most.

4. **Spend regular time in prayer. (Jer. 33:3.)**
   God told Jeremiah that if he would pray and call
   out to Him, that He would answer him, showing
   him great and mighty things that he knows not.
   The Hebrew meaning of that word *mighty* is
   "hidden."[1] Prayer will unlock things in your life
   that could have remained hidden forever.

3 SECRETS TO REAL SUCCESS

There's not a graduate reading this book who doesn't want it—success. You don't want to go out and fail. Success is your goal and God wants to help you attain it. But it is important to define real success so that you know exactly what you're praying for.

1. **Real success is never compared to someone else's achievements.** Your measuring stick for success in your life is not your big brother or best friend. Success for you is based on the talents God has given you and how well you apply them.

2. **Real success is loving God and loving people.** All the money, power, and recognition in the world will not satisfy the deepest yearnings of the human soul. That's why many of the unhappiest people in the world are rich athletes,

entertainers, and entrepreneurs. In the process of reaching our goals, love God and love people.

3. **Real success is long term, not short term. (Matt. 16:26.)** If you succeed by the world's standards for 70 or 80 years but pass from this life into eternity without God, what have you gained? Don't lose your soul while trying to gain in this world.

5 WAYS TO GET A GREAT JOB

I've held a job since I was 12 years old. I've learned how to work hard and have never been fired. I've discovered that if you give your best, you will have the opportunity to eventually do work that you enjoy and get promoted into a really cool job. Here are 5 ways to land a great job or career.

1. Get out into the workplace and hunt your job down. Knock on doors, set up interviews, and learn to sell your desire and ability.

2. Be sure you have properly trained and prepared yourself for the job you really want. If it means college, find a way to get to college. Read, learn, intern, volunteer, and do whatever it takes to become the best in your field.

3. Start out in any company or organization being willing to do the small things that other "big shots" aren't willing to do. It will separate and distinguish you from the pack.

4. Set your sights high. Don't allow your own self-doubt or other people's lack of support stop you from going after your goals. (Mark 11:24.)

5. Pray and trust God to open up the doors super-naturally. He can, and He will. (Jer. 33:3.)

3 KEYS TO SOUND CAREER DECISIONS

The average person in America makes a number of career changes during his lifetime. Sometimes it is for the better, but often it is a result of a pattern of indecisiveness, lack of commitment, and impatience. Here are 3 important keys to sound career decisions.

1. **Realize your work alone will never bring true happiness. (Matt. 6:33.)** Those who seek a career to fill their emptiness will be disappointed. However, if we seek God first, He will give us joy and fulfillment in our work. So before you make a career decision or change, be sure your relationship with Christ is all it should be.

2. **Don't be hasty or impulsive in your decision. (Eccl. 5:2.)** The Word of God exhorts us to be patient and cautious in bringing up a matter to God. In making an important decision

in your life, it is always better to be slow and deliberate in getting to the right choice. This will save you from becoming a spiritual rabbit, jumping from one thing to another with no long-term fruitfulness.

3. **Never leave one assignment without a concrete plan for the next.** I've seen too many people feel "led by the Lord" to quit one thing and then go on to wander aimlessly for months, even years, trying to discover what's next. God is not so "mystical" that He is not "practical." He didn't just lead the Children of Israel out of Egypt, but He told them to go to the Land of Canaan.

6 STEPS TO FINDING FAVOR
IN THE WORKPLACE

God wants to help you succeed in all your work. Your success in your job and career will be a direct result of your ability to get along with people. One of the coolest things in the world is having a job you love and working with people you really like. Here are 6 steps to get you there.

1. Don't treat your boss one way and everyone else a different way. People will see your hypocrisy and resent you.

2. Never cheat your company or business by stealing. I'm not just talking about their products or supplies; this also includes their time. If you're constantly late to work, taking long breaks, or leaving early, it's like stealing money out of the cash register, because "time is money."

3. Don't try to destroy someone at work in order to get that person's position for yourself. It will eventually backfire, and you'll be out!

4. When someone else does a good job at work, compliment the person personally and in front of your boss.

5. Never try to take authority or leadership that hasn't been given to you. Just do your job, and stay out of business that isn't yours.

6. Always give 100 percent. If you can give 110 percent, you were never giving 100 percent in the first place!

6 KEYS TO BEING PROMOTED
BY YOUR BOSS

No one likes to work at a job without being recognized
and even promoted for one's labor. There are reasons
why some people seem to climb the ladder of promotion
and authority, while others remain on the lowest rung.
Here are 6 keys to your promotion at work.

1. Always arrive a few minutes early for work and
   then stay at least a few minutes late.

2. Do not allow personal issues or other relationships at your job to take time or focus away from
   your work.

3. Never complain about your pay. You agreed to
   work for that amount, so be grateful!

4. Ask your boss from time to time if there is anything you can do to improve your performance.

5. Work with your head, not just your hands. Think of ways to do your job more effectively.

6. Don't continually badger your boss with requests for promotions or raises. Let your work do the talking, pray, and trust God; and when the timing is right, ask to speak to your boss, without being demanding.

3 REASONS TO QUIT YOUR JOB

While I believe it is extremely important that you are
steadfast and faithful in your work for an employer, there
are times when you have very legitimate reasons to quit.
Here are at least 3 of those reasons.

1. **Your job requires you to compromise your
   Christian principles.** If your work is causing
   your walk with God to be compromised or dimin-
   ished, it is probably time to quit. Perhaps it
   requires you to constantly miss church. Maybe
   you're being asked to do something that goes
   directly against your beliefs and values. Trust
   God and He will lead you to something better.

2. **Fellow employees are having a negative
   effect on your life. (2 Cor. 6:14.)** The Bible
   instructs us not to be unequally yoked with
   unbelievers. If you are "yoked" together with

unbelievers on your job who are causing you to compromise or suffer temptation that is bringing you down, it's time to change jobs. The Bible says with temptation, God gives a way of escape. (1 Cor. 10:13.) It says to "escape," not stay there and try to overcome it.

3. **The Lord is leading you to something better.** There are times when you may have a good job that is meeting your needs, but God has been preparing you for the next step— something even better. When a season of faith-fulness in one place comes to an end, be obedient to step out to His next assignment for your life.

4 KINDS OF PEOPLE WHO
CONSTANTLY GET FIRED

I have been in the workplace for more than 20 years
and have never been fired from a job. Unfortunately, I
have seen many others suffer this difficult experience.
Most of the time they had no one but themselves to
blame. Many of these people fall into one of the following 4 categories.

1. **Those who cannot receive instruction or
   correction.** Instead of acknowledging their short-
   comings and making the appropriate changes, they
   overflow with pride and refuse to listen.

2. **Those who cause strife in the team.** They
   may be talented and diligent workers, but they
   allow jealousy, competitiveness, and hunger for
   power to sabotage their abilities.

3. **Those who refuse to continue to grow and improve.** These people accept mediocrity and will not pay the price to increase their knowledge and ability to perform at their highest level.

4. **Those who are not truthful.** No matter how talented a person is, the individual cannot help an organization if he or she cannot be trusted.

4 KEYS TO EFFECTIVE
BUDGETING AND SAVING

It's really hard to invest money anywhere if you don't have anything left at the end of each month. It is important to develop a financial plan that will ensure that you have money each month to save and invest. Here are 4 keys to doing that.

1. **Know exactly where you are today.** Make out a list of all your monthly income and all your monthly expenses. The goal is to have more income than expenses!

2. **Determine to live below what you earn.** If you are spending all that you earn (or more!) make a commitment to cut back expenses anywhere necessary. It may mean cutting out your cable TV or cell phone, but do what it takes!

3. **Live by the 10 percent rule.** Create a budget that allows you to put 10 percent of your income into savings or investment every month.

4. **Don't forget the tithe!** Before you pay a bill or make an investment, pay your 10 percent tithes to your local church. God will multiply it back abundantly! (Mal.3:10.)

10 KEY QUESTIONS FOR
SPENDING WISELY

The Bible promises that if we honor God with our possessions and first fruits (the tithe), our barns will be filled with plenty. (Prov. 3:9,10.) In the Old Testament, the barn is a storehouse of savings. If you are going to save effectively, you must spend wisely. Remember, it's not how much you make that counts but how much you have left over when it's all said and done. So here are 10 questions to consider before buying something.

1. Do I really need it?

2. Is the price right?

3. Is it the right time to buy?

4. Is there a substitute for this?

5. Is there any major disadvantage in this purchase?

6. Have I researched the item carefully?

7. Will its value increase/decrease dramatically?

8. Does it complement my Christian testimony?

9. Does it require great expenses in upkeep?

10. Have I sought outside counsel?

3 REASONS YOU SHOULD TITHE

There are really more than 3 reasons you should tithe; but if these don't inspire you to tithe, another 100 reasons won't either.

1. **God says if you don't you're robbing Him. (Mal. 3:10,11.)** This doesn't sound like a very good plan. I'm sure God has a good security system that lets Him know anytime a thief robs Him of His tithes. Do you think God is going to bless a thief who is robbing Him?

2. **God said that if you do what He says, He will flood you with blessings.** It sounds like a good thing to be flooded with blessings. Get your boat ready for God's good flood.

3. **God will work His pest control on anything that will try to attack your finances.** Some

people lose great financial crops because of pests, accidents, theft, and so forth. Use pest control by tithing.

God says, "Test me in this" (Mal. 3:10 NIV). Put Him to the test. Honor Him with your tithes, and watch the blessings flow your way.

4 THINGS YOU SHOULD KNOW
ABOUT INVESTING

God wants you to grow and develop everything He has given you, including your money. In the parable of the talents (actual money in Jesus' time) the master rebukes the servant who does not get interest on the money that was left to him. (Matt. 25:24-26). The Lord wants to help you multiply your finances. With that said, it is important to know these 4 things about successful investing.

1. **Start as early as possible, even in small amounts.** The biggest mistake people make is to wait until they're "older" or "have more money" to start an investment program. A good rule of thumb is to set aside 10 percent of your monthly income into an investment program of some kind.

2. **Get professional help with your invest-ment choices.** Whether you're buying into stocks (ownership in companies), mutual funds (a collection of different stocks), or bonds (a debt security from the government or another organi-zation) be sure to consult with a certified finan-cial planner. Ask around your church. Talk to successful business people. You will find someone who invests for a living and can help you make wise decisions.

3. **Commit to "forced" monthly investing.** Once you choose a good investment vehicle, try to have some kind of automatic draft taken out of either your bank account or paycheck. This way you don't have to make the decision every month. It's done for you and you are less likely to quit!

4. **Don't try to "get rich quick."** Beware of people who have a "guarantee" that your money

will double or triple with an investment. Don't allow someone to pressure you into a "big opportunity" without having the chance to do thorough research and get counsel from trusted friends or colleagues.

3 PLACES FOR SUCCESSFUL INVESTING

In order to grow your money, you are going to have to plant it like a seed in the right soil for it to produce. You must be willing to start small and take one simple step at a time. Remember, "A man's steps (not the running leaps) are directed by the Lord" (Prov. 20:24). Here are 3 places you can successfully invest your money.

1. **In your own business.** This may be the best return you will ever get because you have complete control over all that you do. It may be investing in lawn care equipment for a landscaping business or it could be an investment in a university to become a doctor.

2. **In the stock market.** When you buy stocks, bonds, or mutual funds (collection of stocks), you are basically buying a small part of a company like Wal-Mart, GAP, or General Motors.

You must do very good research, get sound advice from experts, and believe that the stock you buy will grow. Remember this: 9 out of 10 companies fail in 5 years. Of those that survive the first 5 years, 9 out of 10 eventually fail as well.[2] So invest in proven companies that you know will be around a long time.

3. **In a home.** As soon as you can, buy a home after you get out of high school. While your cars and video games will depreciate in value, a home purchased in the right place at the right price will go up in value.

4 REASONS YOU SHOULD BUY A HOUSE

The faster you can get yourself in a position to buy your own house, the better. If you rent or lease you are literally paying for someone else's home. Ten years later you may be out the door with nothing for your money and they have a house that's paid for and has increased in value. It's easier to buy a house today than you might think. Talk to others that own a house and start doing some research in your area. Meet with a good realtor. Here's why:

1. **Property generally appreciates and goes up in value.** Just about everything else you buy will go down in value—cars, jewelry, clothes— but a well-built home in a good area will usually be worth more in 5 years from now. It can become your first major investment vehicle.

2. **You will build equity into your home over the length of the mortgage.** Each month, a part of your mortgage payment is like cash you're putting into your own bank account. You are literally saving money every month. If you can afford to do a 15-year mortgage (higher payments) instead of a 30-year mortgage, you will save even more!

3. **The United States Government allows a housing deduction.** You will save on your tax expenses each year as the government allows you to deduct your mortgage interest payments and property taxes from your federal income tax return. This is good news!

5 WAYS MONEY CAN DESTROY PEOPLE

Movies, and most other media, paint the picture that money is the solution to all your problems. "If you have more money, everything will be better." That is not true. In fact, money, if handled and perceived incorrectly, can destroy people. Here are 5 ways money can destroy in the hands of the wrong person.

1. Money can give a false sense of security. Jesus rebuked the church of Laodicea in Revelation 3:17 because they were cold toward Him, thinking they were okay because they had wealth.

2. Money can cause people to worry about a need for more. Jesus said that our lives do not consist in the abundance of our possessions. (Luke 12:15.)

3. Some people in their greed for more money will
    compromise to gain. What they compromise to
    gain, they will have to compromise to keep; but
    they will eventually lose it all. (Prov. 13:11.)

4. When people have money, they often worry about
    losing it. The money they thought would give
    peace of mind now enslaves them to fear.

5. Love of money can choke God's Word from being
    fruitful in our lives. (Matt. 13:22.)

Money isn't a bad thing. In fact, it can prove to be a
powerful tool for good in the hands of the right person.
Make sure you aren't destroyed by the 5 misconceptions
of money.

7 REWARDS OF THE GIVER

If you think you get the short end of the deal by being a giver, think again. Take a look at these 7 rewards Scripture promises to those who give.

1. You will prosper. (Prov. 11:25.) That's much better than the alternative.

2. You will be refreshed and encouraged by other people. (Prov. 11:25.) We all need this at different points in our lives.

3. You will get back what you give, but it will come back bigger and better. (Luke 6:38.)

4. God personally sees to it that you receive your reward. (Eph. 6:8.)

5. You will be flooded with good things. (Mal. 3:10.)

6. You will have supernatural protection over your finances. (Mal. 3:11.)

7. You will have treasure in heaven that no one can take away. (Luke 18:22.)

Take advantage of the rewards available to you by being a giver. You can watch others be blessed, or you can obey God's Word and receive blessings, too.

[GOD]

4 STEPS TO FINDING FAVOR WITH GOD

Let's be honest. If you can get yourself in favor with the most powerful person in the universe, you're going to do really well. The great thing is that God has told us clearly in His Word that we can fall into favor with Him. Here are 4 steps to getting there.

1. **Diligently seek after Him.** He promises to reward and bless anyone who wholeheartedly seeks Him. (Heb.11:6.)

2. **Search out the wisdom of God's Word.** He promises that when we discover His wisdom we will obtain favor from Him.

3. **Develop a lifestyle of praising God without apology.** The churches in the book of Acts were bold to praise God with their voices and found favor with all the people. (Acts 2:47.)

4. **Walk into goodness and integrity toward others.** God promises you favor but condemns the person who is wicked in one's actions. (Prov. 12:2.)

3 DAILY HABITS TO GROW IN
YOUR RELATIONSHIP WITH GOD

Habits make or break us. In fact, our lives are byproducts of the daily habits we form. Research has said it takes 21 days to form a habit. Take the next 3 weeks to build these 3 habits in your life and watch your walk with God grow.

1. At breakfast each morning read one chapter of Proverbs. By the time you're done eating you will have easily read a chapter.

2. Find one Scripture in the chapter you read that really stands out to you. Write it down on a piece of paper or a 3 x 5 index card and carry it with you wherever you go.

3. Whenever you hit slow times in your day, such as being stuck in traffic, pull out the card and meditate on your Scripture.

Commit these 3 simple habits to your life, and you will grow rapidly.

3 MISTAKES GRADUATES MAKE IN
THEIR WALK WITH GOD

As you begin a brand new season of life it will be important for you to start strong spiritually. Most Christians don't plan to fail in their relationship with God. They just make some simple, sometimes subtle, mistakes that slowly compromise their Christian life. Here are 5 mistakes to be aware of.

1. **They believe the lie that they can keep a strong relationship with God without consistent church attendance. (Heb. 10:25.)** The Word instructs us not to forsake the assembling of ourselves together. Christianity is not an "island" existence. We need one another for encouragement, guidance, and inspiration.

2. **They slip spiritually, accept condemnation, and quit. (Rom. 8:1.)** You are stepping

out on your own for the first time and you will make some mistakes. That is a part of life and a part of growing up. The key is to get back up, ask for help and forgiveness, and keep going. God will grace you to overcome and conquer.

3. **They allow relationships to develop that are not equally yoked spiritually. (2 Cor. 6:14.)** While it's great to have a lot of friends and look for opportunities to share a witness of your faith with non-Christians, it is important to guard your closest friendships. Make a vow before God to keep a godly, Christ-like foundation with your closest friends.

7 SCRIPTURES THAT PROVE
GOD IS CONFIDENT IN YOU

Here are 7 encouraging Scriptures to look up and commit to memory.

1. **Psalm 138:8** God will fulfill His purpose for your life.

2. **John 3:16** God believed in you enough to allow His Son, Jesus, to die for you.

3. **Mark 16:15** After Jesus rose from the dead He gave His ministry to His disciples and us to finish.

4. **Jude 24** He said He would keep you from falling and present you in His presence with great joy.

5. **Acts 1:8** He gave us His power and Holy Spirit to witness.

6. **John 15:16** He handpicked you. You're His first-round draft pick.

7. **Ephesians 2:5** Even while we were lost, He made us alive with Him.

If God is confident in you, that should be enough for you. He is the Creator of the universe, and He is on your side—you can't lose.

3 SECRETS TO ANSWERED PRAYER

If you haven't already, it won't be long before you move
out on your own. Actually, you will never be "on your
own"—God will always be with you. While you may not
have a mother or father there for you all the time, the
Lord will be your provider. The answers you need in
every area of life are just a prayer away. Here are 3
secrets to getting the answers you want.

1. **Learn to pray according to God's will.
   (1 John 5:14.)** God has promised to give you
   anything that He has "willed" to you. His Word is
   His will. Read the Bible carefully, making note of
   the promises of provision, guidance, healing,
   and everything else that belongs to you as a son
   or daughter of God.

2. **Believe that God is a rewarder. (Heb.
   11:6.)** God tells us when we approach Him we

should do so believing not only that He is alive, but that He is ready to reward you when you seek Him. God is a good God and has good things for you. Expect His best every day!

3. **Stand in faith, even when things don't seem to change. (Heb. 11:17.)** Faith believes you have the answers to your prayers even before you see them with your own eyes. After you've prayed for something, begin to thank God that He has heard you and the answer is on the way!

4 WAYS GOD GIVES YOU DIRECTION

Do you need direction? Good, because God wants to give it to you. The direction of God is not hard to come by. Here are 4 ways He will give it to you.

1. **The Word (Bible):** the most practical way that God gives direction. All other ways must line up with this way.

2. **Peace:** how God will lead you. His peace will be deep down inside letting you know you're headed in the right direction.

3. **People:** pastors, teachers, parents, and friends. God will speak through these people whom He has strategically placed in your life.

4. **Desires:** what you want to do. Do you like making art, building, or helping others? God

has placed desires in your heart to help give you direction.

4 REASONS YOU NEED A GOOD PASTOR

The Bible tells us that God has set pastors in the church to help us grow and mature. (Eph. 4:11-15.) Pastors are a gift from God to the church, and it is up to us to allow a pastor to speak into our lives through the Word of God each week. Here are 4 reasons you must have a good pastor.

1. **A good pastor will protect you from wolves.** A good pastor has a shepherd's heart and will warn you, helping you steer clear of people and situations that could destroy you.

2. **A good pastor will feed you.** Without spiritual food you will slowly suffer spiritual malnutrition, losing the strength you need to be victorious every day in life. Each time you sit under God's Word you are feeding on spiritual nutrients.

3. **A good pastor will inspire you.** God will use your pastor to open your heart and mind to the dreams and vision God has for you.

4. **A good pastor will correct you. (2. Tim. 4:2.)** Good pastors are not afraid to bring rebuke and correction that will keep us from getting in a ditch. God will supernaturally lead them to say things that are exactly what you need to hear each week.

5 THINGS GOD SAYS ABOUT WORK

Our work is very important to God. Unfortunately, there are a lot of teenagers who don't think seriously about work until they finish high school or college, but now is the time to develop good work habits in your life. A strong work ethic will virtually ensure success in any career you choose. Here are 5 critical things God's Word has to say about work.

1. If you don't work, you won't eat. (2 Thess. 3:10.) Work is the exchange God has created for all of us to gain finances to provide for our daily needs. God didn't say to pray, hope, or beg—He said to work.

2. We are to work as if our boss is Jesus—not human beings. (Eph. 6:5.) Even when the boss isn't looking, the Lord sees all that you do.

3. Our work should produce good fruit and results. (Col. 1:10.) Don't just put in the time, but learn how to get results.

4. If we're faithful and consistent in the small things in our jobs, we'll be promoted to bigger tasks and responsibilities. (Matt. 25:23.)

5. A worker is worthy of one's pay. (Matt. 10:10.) You should be paid fairly for your work; and once you've agreed on a wage, you have no right to complain about your pay. Be cheerful!

[MARRIAGE]

7 QUALITIES TO LOOK FOR IN
YOUR FUTURE SPOUSE

It's a good idea to know what you really want in a spouse before you begin a relationship. If you wait until you're emotionally involved with someone, your judgment gets clouded and bad decisions are often the byproduct. Many people wake up one day in a marriage they hate because they were not clear on what it was they really wanted. Aim at nothing and you will hit it every time. Here are 7 qualities you should look for in your future spouse.

1. **Equally yoked.** The apostle Paul warned us about being unequally yoked together with unbelievers. (2 Cor. 6:14.) Imagine being tied with a rope to another person while trying to run a race—you want to go west and they want to go east. How far will you get? Make sure this person is going in the same direction spiritually that you are.

2. **Common interests.** It's good for you to have many of the same interests. It could be difficult if you love to be out often, are a world traveler, and like meeting lots of people but your spouse is content to stay home and is quiet and shy. Make sure you both enjoy many of the same things.

3. **Same values.** Does this person have the same values you have? Many relationships hit turbulent times because of sharp disagreements about values. Talk about these before you get too involved.

4. **Like-minded goals.** Do you both want children? Do you want to be wealthy and they are content to get by? What are your goals for your life, marriage, family, and finances? Most of them should be on the same page as yours.

5. **Respect for you.** Respect is a foundational stone for all healthy relationships. Does this

person see your uniqueness and God-given gifts and treat you as special, or is this person spending all his or her time trying to change you?

6. **Character.** Does this person have godly character? Does he or she do what is right, or what is popular and convenient? If you don't have character, you don't have anything.

7. **Attraction.** You should find this person attractive. Serving God and seeking Him first doesn't mean God is going to give you a spouse you are not attracted to. The opposite is true. Serve Him faithfully and He can get you one that is out of your league. He did for me. God wants you to have someone you love inside and out.

3 REASONS FRIENDSHIP IS
MORE IMPORTANT THAN ROMANCE

Romance is a good thing. As a married man, I know.
However, friendship is more important: it should be the
foundation that romance is built on. Let's take a look at
3 reasons friendship is more important than romance.

1.   **Longevity.** Friendship is long lasting. Romance
     is temporary. Romance is defined as a strong,
     usually short-lived, attachment or feeling.
     Friendship is there for the long haul.

2.   **More than a feeling.** It's a fact. The feeling of
     romance will come and go. Romance has a lot to
     do with its environment and circumstances.
     Friendship, on the other hand, is there whether
     we feel it or not.

3. **You can be yourself.** You don't have to worry about impressing others. There is no need for you to present yourself in an unrealistic manner to gain affection. A true friend will still love you when you've had one too many Big Macs.

5 SIGNS THAT YOU MAY BE
READY TO MARRY

How do you know when you are ready to get married?
By society's standards it is being eighteen, having
money for a wedding ceremony, and a willing fiancé.
However, there should be much more than these if you
want a marriage that will last a lifetime. Here are 5 indi-
cators that you might be ready for marriage.

1. **You have a healthy self-esteem.** The Bible
    says we are to love our neighbor as ourselves.
    (Matt. 22:39.) If we don't have a healthy love and
    respect for ourselves, how can we genuinely love
    others? After all, love is the foundation for a
    good marriage.

2. **You are financially responsible.** Learn to be
    good with your money. Arguments over money is
    one of the top causes of divorce. Don't spend

every dime you make. Develop the discipline to
save something each time you get paid—I
suggest 10 percent.

3. **You have developed a good friendship
   with your potential mate.** Marriage is
   about spending the rest of your life with your
   best friend. Marriages that are built on physical
   or romantic whirlwinds usually don't last.
   Friendship is the foundation for a love that
   lasts forever.

4. **You and your potential spouse are in
   agreement about your values, dreams,
   and goals.** Too often people spend all their
   time planning their wedding and honeymoon and
   never ask the real questions. Is this person I am
   about to marry going the same direction I am in
   life? Amos 3:3 asks the important question, "Can
   two walk together, unless they are agreed?"

5. **You are prepared to live the rest of your life with this person just the way he or she is.** Many people marry someone thinking they can change what they don't like about them after they get married. What if they never change? Can you live the rest of your life with their habits, quirks, and attitudes that drive you nuts? If they drive you nuts now, they will drive you insane later.

3 THINGS MARRIAGE WILL DO FOR YOU

Marriage is a wonderful thing. I have been happily married for almost twenty-five years to my wife, Cathy, and our marriage gets better every day. That isn't to say we haven't had our moments, but we work through them and our love and understanding for one another continues to grow. Here are 3 things that marriage has done for me and will also do for you.

1. **Marriage gives you a great understanding of God's love.** In fact, the Bible says that the Church is Christ's bride and He loved her and laid down His life for her. (Eph. 5:25.) One thing I have learned is that there isn't anything I wouldn't do to protect my wife from harm. The love I have for her would compel me to lay my life down for her if I needed to. This has really given me a clearer picture of how much God loves me.

2. **Marriage teaches you how to love uncon-
ditionally.** Many of today's marriages are
ending in divorce because they have grown tired
of one another and they want something new and
fresh. The wedding vows don't say "until I get
tired of you" or "until someone better looking
comes along." It says, "until death do us part."
Marriage is about loving one another through the
good times and the bad times. And the bad times
can get pretty bad. But if you walk in uncondi-
tional love, the rewards of a great marriage will
be worth it. Then the good times will far outweigh
any of the bad ones.

3. **Marriage teaches you to respect each
other's differences.** This is such an important
skill to learn in life because there isn't anyone
else exactly like you. Marriage is about respect-
ing and enjoying one another's differences rather
than trying to mold them into your image. My

wife's strengths balance my weaknesses and my strengths balance her weaknesses. Learning to enjoy the differences in one another will help make a life-long marriage great.

3 THINGS MARRIAGE WON'T DO FOR YOU

Since we were little children we've watched the movies about the fairy tale marriage where the prince and princess ride off into the sunset and live happily ever after. Marriage is made to look like the solution to all life's problems. Few people ever stop to think about what marriage will not and cannot do for them. It is important that you don't enter into this life commitment with unrealistic expectations that cannot be fulfilled through marriage. This will only lead to frustration and disillusionment.

Here are 3 things marriage will not do for you.

1. **Remove sexual temptation from your life.**
   We live in a sex-saturated society. It's all over the TV, billboards, and movies—it's everywhere. Even in marriage you will have to keep your thoughts submitted to the Word of God regarding sex. Adultery happens in many marriages

because someone doesn't keep their sex drive under the control of God's Word. David said, "Your word I have hidden in my heart, That I might not sin against You" (Ps. 119:11).

2. **Eliminate loneliness.** God is the only one that can truly fill the relationship hole in your heart. When we learn to be satisfied by His presence then we will truly be able to enjoy the company of others.

3. **Fix all your problems.** Many people think that marriage is the cure for all their problems. However, the opposite is true. If you are not able to handle the problems you have now, you aren't ready for marriage. Marriage is the merging together of your problems with your spouse's problems. Thus, you have more problems. That isn't bad because you now have the both of you to work on them; however, you must be ready for

this new pressure. The bottom line is that marriage can be great but it isn't the solution to all your problems.

Realizing the things marriage cannot do and putting your trust in God to make up the difference is a great step towards living the "happily ever after" dream.

4 HABITS OF A HAPPY MARRIAGE

Habits make us what we are. If we form good habits we will have good success. But if we develop poor habits we will suffer the consequences. Winners form winning habits just as losers form losing habits. Here are 4 habits of winning marriages.

1. **Never stop dating your spouse.** When people are dating they can hardly wait until the next time they can go out with each other. From the time the date is over they are planning their next date. It consumes their thoughts. Happy marriages never stop dating. They make it a regular part of their life.

2. **Keep doing the little things.** Before marriage we work hard and are creative at winning the affection of the one we love—notes, flowers, candies, poems, and so on. But after marriage

many people feel that they have won their prize and they can stop the pursuit. Never stop doing the things you did to win their affection. Keep doing the little things that say, "I love you."

3. **Never go to bed mad at each other.** Every marriage has moments of anger towards one another for various reasons. This is a part of relationships. The Bible warns us not to let the sun go down on our anger. (Eph. 4:26.) Often our natural reaction to arguments is to go to bed mad at each other and get even with the silent treatment. This only gives the devil a foothold in your marriage. (Eph. 4:27.) Work out your differences. Don't be too proud to say, "I was wrong. Please forgive me." It is better to be wrong and still be married in your twilight years than to be right and die a lonely divorced person.

4. **Faithful church attendance.** The happiest marriages are the ones that build their life around God rather than trying to fit God into their life. If you try to fit God into your life there will always be a reason you can't go to church this time but you will next time. And so on and so on. Happy marriages put God and the church first.

7 ABSOLUTES OF GOD'S WILL
FOR YOUR LIFE

Have you ever heard someone say, "God moves in mysterious ways"? I sure am glad that statement isn't true. The will of God doesn't have to be mysterious. Here are 7 things you can absolutely count on.

1. **God's will is salvation.** Our heavenly Father desires that all of humankind have eternal life with Him. That includes you.

2. **God's will is dominion.** Dominion simply means control. God wants you to apply His Word and take control of your body, thought life, attitude, and future.

3. **God's will is discipleship.** We are to grow in our walk with Christ. As we mature, we are to help others do the same.

4. **God's will is unity.** Your words and actions must be united with God's Word.

5. **God's will is stewardship.** We are to take proper care of our time, money, abilities, and all God has entrusted us with.

6. **God's will is relationships.** Through the power of relationships, you will be able to accomplish things that would be impossible if you were alone.

7. **God's will is progressive.** God has a plan for your life that will be completed one step at a time, not in leaps or bounds.

5 SIGNS OF A CONFIDENT PERSON

Use this as a check to see if you are confident in who you are in Christ.

1. You aren't afraid to meet new people.

2. You like to try new things and see new places.

3. You aren't afraid to take calculated risks in order to achieve something you want.

4. You don't get discouraged and depressed when you fail. Instead, you pick yourself back up.

5. It doesn't bother you much when people criticize you.

If all of the statements above describe you, you are very confident. If 4 of the statements are true about you, your confidence is solid and improving. Three true statements mean you could use some improvement. It's not looking good if only 2 statements are true; you are limiting yourself from great experiences. If you only found 1 statement to be true, reread this book every day until all the statements are true. Remember, in Christ you are a new creation. (2 Cor. 5:17.)

[CHALLENGES]

3 THINGS TO DO WHEN YOU FAIL

Everyone fails. When you do, it is important that you realize failing doesn't make you a failure. Failure is falling down and refusing to get back up. How about the first time you tried to walk. What happened? You fell. But you didn't stay down; you got back up. You probably fell again and again, but you continued to get back up and try until you mastered the art of walking. The Bible is packed full of stories about great men and women of God who fell at different times but they continued to get back up. As a result God was able to use them to accomplish great things. Here are 3 things that will help you get back up on your feet when you fail.

1. **Admit your failure.** When Adam and Eve disobeyed God and ate the forbidden fruit, they tried to cover their sin by hiding from God. Proverbs 28:13 says that whoever covers his sin will not prosper. God asked Adam if he had eaten the for-

bidden fruit and Adam shifted the blame to Eve.
Eve then blamed the serpent. (Gen. 3:11-13.)
When you sin, ask God to forgive you and He
will. (1 John 1:9.)

2. **Learn from your mistake.** Henry Ford made
over 10,000 unsuccessful attempts before developing the incandescent light bulb. Every unsuccessful experiment narrowed down the
possibilities until he found the right one. A sci-
entist once said, "In science mistakes always
precede the truth." When you learn from your
mistakes they can become stepping-stones to a
brighter future.

3. **Don't repeat it.** When you learn what caused
you to fall, you now have the power not to repeat
it. Was your fall the result of a poor relationship
you need to change? Maybe it was the result of
ignoring the advice of others because you have

an unteachable spirit. Whatever it may be you can close the door to future failure by learning from past mistakes. One man said it well when he penned, "We cannot rewrite the past, but we can write the future."

The good news is that in God our past mistakes don't have to be a prophecy about our future. God is always the God of new beginnings.

4 WAYS TO DEAL WITH A "JERK"

Most likely you have already encountered a jerk some-time in your life. If you haven't, don't worry, you will eventually—most likely sooner than later. When you do there are four things you should keep in mind.

1. **See them through the eyes of God's love.**
   Ask yourself what it is in their life or past that is driving them to be this way. When people are insensitive and hurt other people it is because they themselves are hurting. When you realize hurting people hurt people it helps you to see them through God's eyes of compassion.

2. **Forgive them just as God has forgiven you.** The Bible is very clear that we must forgive those who offend us. In the Lord's Prayer, Jesus taught us to pray, "forgive us our debts as we also have forgiven our debtors" (Matt. 6:12 NIV).

Jesus went even further to say that if we don't forgive those who offend us that God won't forgive us either. (Matt. 6:15 NIV.) However, forgiveness doesn't mean we hang around and let people walk all over us. We should protect ourselves and do what we can to avoid physically, emotionally, and spiritually harmful people.

3. **Don't toss fuel on the fire.** Many times when we encounter a real first-class jerk our first reaction is to put them in their place and give them a real piece of our mind. Here is some good advice. Keep all the pieces of your mind to yourself—you are going to need all of them later in life. Secondly, anything you say or do is most likely going to cause things to get worse. Proverbs 15:1 says, "A soft answer turns away wrath, but a harsh word stirs up anger." Don't stir up strife. Put the lid on the gas can by keeping your mouth shut.

4. **Follow God's plan of revenge.** Romans
    12:19-20 NIV says, "Do not take revenge, my
    friends, but leave room for God's wrath, for it is
    written: 'It is mine to avenge; I will repay,' says
    the Lord. On the contrary: 'If your enemy is
    hungry, feed him; if he is thirsty, give him some-
    thing to drink. In doing this, you will heap
    burning coals on his head.'" Doing kind things
    to those who are jerks is the last thing they
    expect and the last thing they want. It takes all
    the joy they have out of being mean to you. God
    will use your kindness to bring conviction into
    their life and it will be a great witness of God's
    love. Remember, you are the only Jesus people
    ever see.

Jerks aren't fun to be around, but you have the power to
be the bigger person as you yield yourself to God's love.

6 KEYS TO GETTING ALONG
WITH A ROOMMATE

Most people will have at least one roommate in life, and
if you don't you will most likely get married and live
with your spouse. So, here are some good tips to
getting along with your roommate or spouse.

1. **Establish the house rules.** Most arguments
    that occur are misunderstandings because the
    rules were not clearly defined. So sit down with
    them and write out the rules of the house. What
    are the rules about picking up after yourself,
    bringing guests over, cooking meals, the gro-
    ceries, and the volume of the TV late at night.

2. **Respect each other's stuff.** Most fights that
    occur are the result of not respecting each other's
    personal belongings or space. Don't use your
    roommate's new sweater without permission, or

drink their last can of coke. Remember the golden rule of having a roommate and you will eliminate many arguments: "Do unto your roommate's stuff as you would have them do unto yours."

3. **Don't let your frustrations build up.** Jesus teaches us in Matthew to talk to those who offend us. (Matt. 18:15.) Rather than letting it build up or gossip to others about it, we must work it out with the person who offends us. Most of the time it was a simple misunderstanding and your relationship will become stronger because you dealt with it. Relationships take work, lots of work, but they are worth it.

4. **Prefer them above yourself.** Paul wrote to the Philippians that we are to be like Christ and prefer others above ourselves. (Phil. 2:3-5.) Don't always think about what you want. Stop and think about the needs of your roommate and

put them above your own. If you do this you will be amazed to see the difference it will make in the way your roommate treats you. According to Galatians 6:7 whatever a man sows, that is what he will reap.

5. **Don't focus on the little things.** It is amazing how most arguments happen over little things that make no difference in eternity, or even in this life for that matter. Stop, take a step back, and ask yourself if this will really matter a month from now or even at the end of the day.

6. **Give them space for themselves.** Everyone needs time to be alone. Respect your roommate's need for privacy. Before you have guests come over, call and see if it is okay. Little gestures of thoughtfulness like this will go a long way to building lasting friendships you can enjoy for years to come.

5 SUREFIRE WAYS TO MAKE NEW FRIENDS IN A NEW PLACE

A new place can often be intimidating and lonely. But it can also be a great adventure if you take the initiative to meet new people. Even if you are naturally a shy person, if you follow these simple steps you will find it easy to make new friends.

1. **Take advantage of every opportunity to introduce yourself to people.** Introduce yourself to people in the school bookstore, cafeteria, library, and in class. The more people you meet the greater the odds you will find people you really connect with.

2. **Remember to use people's names.** There is no better sound to a person than his or her own name. If you aren't good at remembering names, here is a little trick that will help. When

you introduce yourself and your new acquaintance gives you their name be sure to use it right away. For example, "Fred, it sure is good to meet you. Fred, what classes do you have this semester?" If you can use their name at least three times in your conversation you will be more likely to remember their name. They will also be impressed the next time you see them and use their name.

3. **Ask them questions about themselves.**

Your conversation will be a hit because you are talking about their favorite subject—them! Everyone's favorite subject is themselves. It is often said, God gave us two ears and one mouth because He wants us to do twice as much listening as talking. A university study has found that good listening can be worth as much as 20 IQ points. I'll take all the extra points I can get!

4. **Have good eye contact.** If your eyes are always wandering during your conversation, people will feel you are uninterested in them. Also, poor eye contact can send them the message you are insecure or you are hiding something from them.

5. **Be selective when choosing your closest friends.** Close friends are people that influence your values, self-esteem, and dreams. Be careful to choose friends who love God like you, believe in your dreams, and build you up. If they are always tearing you down you can do something about it—get some new friends. A famous mathematician once said, "You have to have seven positives to overcome one negative." Life is too short to waste it with people who don't believe in you.

7 THINGS TO REMEMBER
WHEN STARTING OVER

Everyone has felt the need to start over with a clean slate more than once in their life. Here are some simple steps that will make starting over a success.

1. **Forgive yourself.** When we confess our sins to God He forgives and cleanses us. (1 John 1:9.) David wrote in Psalm 103:12 that, "as far as the east is from the west, so far has He removed our transgressions from us." If God forgives and forgets our sins when we ask, we should also forgive ourselves. Sometimes we feel that if we mope around and punish ourselves for our sin that it will make us feel better. Jesus already took the punishment for our sin. You just need to receive God's forgiveness by faith and get on with your life.

2. **Learn from your mistake.** Did you get into this bad situation because of poor decisions in your friendships, entertainment choices, or wrong priorities? If you can identify the root cause you can make changes to avoid this again in the future. Everyone makes mistakes but to keep making the same one over is just plain stupid.

3. **Focus on your future not your past.** Paul said, "…forgetting what is behind and straining toward what is ahead" (Phil. 3:13b NIV). You can't live in the present if you are always thinking about your past. You can't rewrite yesterday but you can write a new story today.

4. **Build healthy relationships.** When starting over it is good to evaluate if we have the healthy relationships we need. Healthy relationships will give the emotional and moral support you need to change and build over. Proverbs 27:17 NIV

says, "As iron sharpens iron, so one man sharpens another." Pick your friends carefully. Look for ones that build you, believe in you, and back you up.

5. **Set yourself clear goals.** Proverbs 29:18 KJV says, "Where there is no vision, the people perish." If you aim at nothing you will hit it every time. Nothing great was ever achieved without vision. Dream about what you want in your relationships, finances, career, and relationship with God.

6. **Put them in writing.** The Bible tells us in Habakkuk 2:2 to "Write the vision and make it plain on tablets, that he may run who reads it." Put your vision in writing and make it so clear that it gives you the momentum to run toward your dreams. Maybe you want to lose 10 pounds, or retire by 50 years old, or become a black belt.

Whatever your goals, put them in writing and post them where you can see them every day to help you run toward the things that really matter to you.

7. **Take steps.** Many of your goals may be long-term and seem hard to achieve. Don't try to take leaps toward your dreams but rather take steps. Proverbs 20:24 says, "A man's steps are of the Lord." You don't eat a steak in one big bite—you eat it one bite at a time.

5 OBSTACLES YOU MUST OVERCOME
TO GROW FINANCIALLY

The Bible is clear that God delights in the prosperity of His servants. (Ps. 35:27.) Yet many of His children do not prosper in the area of their finances. They have allowed at least 1 of 5 major obstacles to stand in their way of financial success.

1. **Fear.** Perhaps our greatest enemy is fear. Satan is the author of all fear, and too many Christians are afraid to take simple steps of faith with their money.

2. **Doubt.** Many Christians believe God wants to bless others, but not them. Faith comes by hearing and hearing by the Word of God (Rom. 10:17), so speak God's Word boldly concerning your money.

3. **Laziness.** You will not gain in your finances if you do not have a diligent hand. You must work hard for God to bless you.

4. **Arrogance.** First Peter 5:5 says that God resists the proud. God will resist blessing you if you remain proud and unwilling to be taught.

5. **Greed.** If you are constantly grabbing and hold everything you get with a tight fist, then you will block His future provision.

7 REWARDS OF A DILIGENT WORKER

Many people seek to do the least they possibly have to at a job. What they fail to understand is that they are blocking the blessings of God from coming their way. Proverbs 21:5 assures us that the plans of the diligent will lead to plenty, while those who are hasty in their work will find poverty. Here are 7 rewards of the diligent worker.

1. **Promotion.** Hard work will be rewarded with higher positions of responsibility.

2. **Recognition.** A diligent person will stand out from the crowd, acknowledged by many.

3. **Wealth.** Companies and organizations will pay good money to those who do their job well.

4. **Respect.** You will gain esteem from your friends, your family, your peers, and your community.

5. **Opportunity.** You will find yourself becoming very valuable to others who will open new doors for you to walk through.

6. **Influence.** You will earn the privilege of teaching, training, and mentoring those who will want to learn from your success.

7. **Fulfillment.** You'll never have to live with regrets, wondering what you could have accomplished if you had only given your best.

6 KEYS TO GETTING THE
MOST OUT OF YOUR TIME

Time is a commodity that can never be replaced. If you lose money or a possession, you can always get it back, but you can never turn back time. The Bible tells us to "redeem," or make the very most of, the time we have. (Eph. 5:16.) Here's how:

1. Appreciate the value of your time. You only get 86,400 seconds a day. Use them well.

2. Set priorities. Remember these words from Zig Ziglar: "You can't do everything you want to do, but you can do anything you want to do."[3]

3. Plan your daily and weekly schedule. Write it down.

4. Don't allow unnecessary interruptions and time-wasters to steal valuable time from your projects.

5. Politely hang up on telemarketers!

6. Learn to delegate things that other people can and will do for you. You can't create more time, but you can use the time of others.

ENDNOTES

[1] Matthew Henry's Commentary on the Whole Bible, Volume 1, Hendrickson Publishers, s.v. "mighty."

[2] Kiyosaki, Robert T. *Rich Dad—Poor Dad,* Warner Books, 2000, p. 82.

[3] Ziglar, Zig. *Top Performance—How to Develop Excellence in Yourself and Others,* Berkley Publishing Group, 1991.

PRAYER OF SALVATION

God loves you—no matter who you are, no matter what your past. God loves you so much that He gave His one and only begotten Son for you. The Bible tells us that "…whoever believes in him shall not perish but have eternal life" (John 3:16 NIV). Jesus laid down His life and rose again so that we could spend eternity with Him in heaven and experience His absolute best on earth. If you would like to receive Jesus into your life, say the following prayer out loud and mean it from your heart.

> Heavenly Father, I come to You admitting that I am a sinner. Right now, I choose to turn away from sin, and I ask You to cleanse me of all unrighteousness. I believe that Your Son, Jesus, died on the cross to take away my sins. I also believe that He rose again from the dead so that I might be forgiven of my sins and made righteous through faith in Him. I call upon the name of Jesus Christ to be the Savior and Lord of my life. Jesus, I choose to follow You and ask that You fill me with the power of the Holy Spirit. I declare that right now I am a child of God. I am free from sin and full of the righteousness of God. I am saved in Jesus' name. Amen.

If you prayed this prayer to receive Jesus Christ as your Savior for the first time, please contact us on the web at www.harrisonhouse.com to receive a free book.

Or you may write to us at

Harrison House

P.O. Box 35035

Tulsa, Oklahoma 74153

MEET BLAINE BARTEL

Past: Came to Christ at age 16 on the heels of the Jesus movement. While in pursuit of a professional freestyle skiing career, answered God's call to reach young people. Developed and hosted ground-breaking television series *Fire by Nite*. Planted and pastured a growing church in Colorado Springs.

Present: Serves under his pastor and mentor of nearly 20 years, Willie George, senior pastor of 12,000-member Church on the Move in Tulsa, Oklahoma. Youth pastor of Oneighty®, America's largest local church youth ministry, and reaches more than 2,000 students weekly. National director of Oneighty's® worldwide outreaches, including a network of over 400 affiliated youth ministries. Host of Elevate, one of the largest annual youth leadership training conferences in the nation. Host of *Thrive*™, youth leader audio resource series listened to by thousands each month.

Passion: Summed up in 3 simple words: "Serving America's Future." Life quest is "to relevantly introduce the person of Jesus Christ to each new generation of young people, leaving footprints for future leaders to follow."

Personal: Still madly in love with his wife and partner of 20 years, Cathy. Raising 3 boys who love God, Jeremy—18, Dillon—16, and Brock—13. Avid hockey player and fan, with a rather impressive Gretzky memorabilia collection.

To contact Blaine Bartel,

write:

Blaine Bartel

Serving America's Future

P.O. Box 691923

Tulsa, OK 74169

www.blainebartel.com

*Please include your prayer requests
and comments when you write.*

To contact Oneighty®, write:

Oneighty®
P.O. Box 770
Tulsa, OK 74101
www.Oneighty.com

OTHER BOOKS BY BLAINE BARTEL

Ten Rules of Youth Ministry and Why Oneighty®

Breaks Them All

every teenager's
little black book
on sex and dating

every teenager's
little black book
on cool

every teenager's
little black book
on cash

every teenager's
little black book
of hard to find information

Additional copies of this book
are available from your local bookstore.

If this book has been a blessing to you
or if you would like to see more of the
Harrison House product line,
please visit us on our website at
www.harrisonhouse.com

HARRISON HOUSE
Tulsa, Oklahoma 74153

THE HARRISON HOUSE VISION

Proclaiming the truth and the power
Of the Gospel of Jesus Christ
With excellence;

Challenging Christians to
Live victoriously,
Grow spiritually,
Know God intimately.